✦✦ SING THIS ONE BACK TO ME ✦✦

Sing This One Back to Me

✦✦WITH SPECIAL GUEST APPEARANCE BY PAPA SUSSO✦✦

BOB HOLMAN

COFFEE HOUSE PRESS
Minneapolis
2013

COFFEE HOUSE PRESS books are available to the trade through our primary distributor, Consortium Book Sales & Distribution, cbsd.com or (800) 283-3572. For personal orders, catalogs, or other information, write to: info@coffeehousepress.org.

Coffee House Press is a nonprofit literary publishing house. Support from private foundations, corporate giving programs, government programs, and generous individuals helps make the publication of our books possible. We gratefully acknowledge their support in detail in the back of this book. To you and our many readers around the world, we send our thanks for your continuing support.

Good books are brewing at coffeehousepress.org

LIBRARY OF CONGRESS CIP INFORMATION
Holman, Bob, 1948–
Sing this one back to me : poems / by Bob Holman.
p. cm.
ISBN 978-1-56689-325-1 (pbk.)
I. Title.
PS3558.035588S56 2013
811'.54—DC23
2012036528

FIRST EDITION | FIRST PRINTING
PRINTED IN THE U.S.A.

Dedication

*With regard to publishing, the clay tablets had tremen-
dous charm. But cuneiform gave way to scrolls and alpha-
betic forms of writing. The papyrus scrolls gave way to
parchment, then to books as we know them. Then finally
Gutenberg came along with moveable type, inde-
pendently reinventing printing, which had already been
invented in Korea and spread throughout Asia. But at
each stage, a little bit of charm was lost and greater
access was gained.*

—ALLAN KORNBLUM

If it weren't for Allan Kornblum, this book would not exist.

We'd certainly discussed it long enough—when did we read together
at the Body Politic in Chicago, Allan? Must have been '71 or '72. Ted
Berrigan, Alice Notley, Bill Knott in the audience, Richard Friedman,
Darlene Pearlstein, Peter Kostakis at the helm. Rose Lesniak, Barg and
Chassler, Bob Rosenthal and Shelly Kraut. That was the reading where
I took off my pants five times, each time to reveal another pair
beneath. I mean, anybody can pile on the sweaters, shirts, T-shirts. Yet
my performance didn't stop Allan from saying the poems he'd heard
would make a good book. And here 'tis.

I have written some books in the intervening years, usually around
projects or collaborations. But the immediacy and collaborative ener-
gies of performance and activism, making CDs and poem films, has
more often been more my milieu. Don't get me wrong—I love books!
Super packaging for info and art. Treasures. Come see my library! But
what Allan has always envisioned, and what he's steered this book into,
is something lovely: a collection of poems, punto.

From the start Allan was an old-school, hands-on editor. "Let me see
all of 'em," he said. So I boxed up a little over a thousand pages and
shipped it to him. The monster in a box (as Spalding Gray called his

manuscript) arrived just before I flew to Minneapolis—we were going to work side by side, rassle those poems into manuscripts. Unlike Jack Spicer, who always said he didn't write poems, he wrote books, I do. I write poems. And here was most everything I'd written in the last ten years.

Allan spread the pages around his living room as if deploying the pieces of a giant jigsaw puzzle. He found themes, put like with like. It was Labor Day Weekend; Cinda wouldn't go in there, Allan wore his bathrobe. For breaks, we went to the Minnesota State Fair a couple times, always having something new on a stick—walleye-on-a-stick, porkchop-on-a-stick, cheese-curds-on-a-stick, mashed-potatoes-on-a-stick. Meanwhile, the poems found their way into a couple dozen piles.

Then Allan applied the Method—we looked through the piles, finding ones that would be great leadoffs for that theme, or maybe for the book. Next we looked for poems that could follow that poem and so—forth! Forth we went, and two or maybe three manuscripts is what we ended up with. *Sing This One Back to Me* is the first to be realized.

After that, I resisted as much as I could every step of the way—up to and including crowd-sourcing the title. How else could I prove to Allan that *I Wrote Money But I Meant Crocodile* was the greatest title ever? Turns out 90 percent of my Twitter/Facebook/Tumblr connections agreed with him. Did the themes hold up? They did—painting and poetry; Papa Susso's poems and orality; dailiness poems about my family. Should the order of the themes be switched? (Yes) Wouldn't the cover look better in magenta (my idea)? No, magentizing the cover was another bad idea—we stick with the colors of the Gambian flag.

Having a great editor not only made the book possible, but infected the poems too, sharpened them like pencils writing themselves. To balance the idea that the book is dedicated to a text man when it so often references orality, let me give a few shoutouts here to those who helped in the creation-via-performance of many of these poems, poets mainly from the "spoken word universe." Shout outs to:

Caroline Casey and Linda Koutsky at Coffee House for a great cover, and to pals Edwin Torres and Elizabeth Castagna, who did some marvelous tweaking;

My griot/teacher Alhaji Papa Susso and the whole Susso/Sissoko clan of West Africa;

Ram Devineni, whose vision and intuitive sense of poetry has changed everything I thought I knew;

Julian Kytasty, ace bandura player, who introduced me to Ukrainian dumy;

Nora Balaban, Banning Eyre, and the rest of Timbila, the Zimbabwean-inspired band, who heard in my words what I'd been hearing in their music;

the Braja Waldman band in Montreal, and Vito Ricci and His Orchestra in Maspeth;

Joy Harjo, Cristin O'Keefe Aptowicz, Nikhil Melnuchuk, David Grubin, and Dewi Prysor, for personal levitation sessions;

and of course hip hoppers, slammers, and spoken word poets of all performance stripes, the Endangered Language activists, and all who have graced the Bowery Poetry Club.

And finally, thanks to Sophie, Nick, Daisy, Mike, Dakota, Lisanne, Anthony, August, Stuart, Kay, Liam, Rory, Moose, and the rest of the mishpucha, which always includes Elizabeth.

Contents

✦✦✦✦✦✦✦✦✦✦✦✦✦✦✦✦✦✦✦✦✦✦✦✦✦✦✦✦✦✦✦✦

✦✦✦✦✦✦✦✦✦✦✦✦✦✦✦✦✦✦✦✦✦✦✦✦✦✦✦✦✦✦✦✦

Van Gogh's Violin
(or, Painters! Poets!)

✦✦✦✦✦✦✦✦✦✦✦✦✦✦✦✦✦✦✦✦✦✦✦✦✦✦✦✦✦✦✦✦

✦✦✦✦✦✦✦✦✦✦✦✦✦✦✦✦✦✦✦✦✦✦✦✦✦✦✦✦✦✦✦✦

Jeliya!
(or, Griot Poems, As Sung by Papa Susso to Bob Holman)

✦✦✦✦✦✦✦✦✦✦✦✦✦✦✦✦✦✦✦✦✦✦✦✦✦✦✦✦✦✦✦✦

✦✦✦✦✦✦✦✦✦✦✦✦✦✦✦✦✦✦✦✦✦✦✦✦✦✦✦✦✦✦✦✦✦

Memory Made Real
(or, You Are No Longer Here to Wash Your Hair)

✦✦✦✦✦✦✦✦✦✦✦✦✦✦✦✦✦✦✦✦✦✦✦✦✦✦✦✦✦✦✦✦✦

✦✦✦✦✦✦✦✦✦✦✦✦✦✦✦✦✦✦✦✦✦✦✦✦✦✦✦✦✦✦✦

[Title of Poem]

Body of poem

Tail of poem

Refrain from poem

Poem coda

Reprise

Surprise rereprise

Tale of tailing off a poem

Cup of tea après poem

Neverending poem, the other poem, yet another poem

Poem behind the poem

Shadow of poem

That ol' poem again

The Poem

Fuck Off, I'm a Fuckin' Welsh Fuckin' Learner!
(That's the title)

I feel like the Red Dragon in the Middle of Battle
Stupid American poet in the middle of the Stomp
Want an apology? No possibility!
My address? The contradiction of definition
Definition Demolition

And you know why?
I'll tell you why!
Cause I'm a Fuckin' Welsh Fuckin' Learner, that's why

Old River Boatman Death, he knows it
What art thou and I, Brother
But a uniform of bones and flesh

The above lines stolen on your behalf from R. Williams Parry &
     TH Parry Williams in the name of American Imperialism!

LADIES AND GENTLEMEN!
My first line of cynghanedd!

"Shaking in my bones"

It's true you know
I AM "shaking in my bones"!
And do you know why?
Because I'm a fuckin' Welsh fuckin' learner
That's fuckin' why!

Baby baby the only way to stop
This poem is to kiss kiss
Where each kiss becomes a word—in Welsh—
In My Big Head of Dreams

Ffwciwch Oma, Dwin Ffwcin' Dysgwr Ffwcin' Gymraeg! (Dyna'r teitl)

Rwy'n teimlo fel y ddraig goch yng nghanol y frwydr
Bardd Americanaidd tumffat yng nghanol y Stomp
Eisiau ymddiheuriad? Dim posibiliad!
Eisiau nghyfeiriad? Dyna ddiffiniad o wrthddywediad
A distrywio'r diffiniad

A dach chi'n gwybod pam?
Mi dduda'i thach chi pam!
Achos mod i'n Ffwcin' Dysgwr Ffwcin' Gymraeg, dyna pam

Hen Gychwr Afon Angau, mae o'n gwbod
Beth ydwyt ti a minnau, frawd
Ond swp o esgyrn mewn gwisg o gnawd

Dygwyd y llinellau uchod ar eich cyfer oddi ar R. Williams Parry a
TH Parry Williams yn enw Imperialaeth Americanaidd!

FONEDDIGION A BONEDDIGESAU!
Fy llinell gyntaf o gynghanedd!

"Yn ysgwyd yn fy esgyrn"

Mae'n wir wyddoch chi
Dwi YN "ysgwyd yn fy esgyrn"!
A dach chi'n gwbod pam?
Achos fy mod i'n ffwcin' dysgwr ffwcin' Gymraeg
Dyna ffwcin' pam!

Baby baby yr unig ffordd o atal y gerdd hon
Yw cusanu cusanu
Lle mae pob cusan yn dod—yn air Cymraeg—
Yn fy mhen a'i lond o freuddwydion

Van Gogh's Violin

(OR, PAINTERS! POETS!)

CALM

Goes up in smoke
Skates the ceiling
Calls for a glass
Of solid glass glass

And when it doesn't come
To ring ring ring
Words themselves articulate
Form the meaning "I'll drink
To that" evaporation

CONNECTION

Something something
Rowing a Green Line
Wake up and it is morning

Van Gogh's Violin

GOOD

Good morning, Vincent
It is early May, 1889
Time to get up and paint
Wheat Field with Rising Sun
Hurry before all the firmament
Starts to fall apart again
Right now it's all singing
"Good morning, Vincent!"

YES YET

This remarkable day
Goes between
Because I paint it
With me in it

PERFECTLY GREAT

It would be great
To eat an apple
But there in the tree
It is perfect

PARTICLE BEARD

Flesh covers face
Wheat covers field

CLOSE-UP

My nose sticks out
    A doorknob
As my poor ear grows
Like a worm back to my head

A crack, that is my brow
And yesterday is my lips
And my teeth are rocks
    I walk on

MISANTHROPE, OR . . .

Shy of people
Friend to star in sky
Where am I?
In a park watching children
Play without thinking

PAINT TOUNGE

I cannot stop
To think

DETAIL

Black bites deeper
Spitting red beside my bed
Struggling through deep forest
Limb line limn time
It's all detail! Everything!

HEIGHTENED WITH WHITE CHALK

Running chalk over my lips
Ecstasy directly transmitted
To grass blade after blade

INTERRUPT DREAM

All joy of LIFE flashes
Blinding revelation green
Simply morning, all the
Racket, all the LANGUAGE
Broken dream pours in
Nothing holds blue
Corners of REALITY
As I reach out, brush
One more tree in the garden
Under the masterful Sun

IT'S IMPORTANT

To put up with everything
As you get it down on paper

LAST PASS

Plow down the sun
Second wind, Old Bay
Last pass on this acre
Go home, go home
Wait—gold. More gold!

POTATO IN SKY

The back of the shed
Needs painting
What next!

PLYING MY TRADE

If I sit here long enough
Maybe I'll figure out what it is

SHEAVES OF WHEAT

There is no stopping now
What I want is everything
And everything is arriving
At once to me

LIFE

Blend foreground
    in background
Temperance in the midst
    of ecstasy
Ha. Lalala. Fill up
Holes with death

VIOLIN

Write everything down
Throw everything away

SUNSET

This morning I raised my eye
And saw the stars
Had not moved
Sweet Death, my Love,
I will never lose you again

Rothkos

RESOLUTE DARK

Blue old leak
Seed green pop
Earth hold brown

SHATTER LOVE

Magenta fire breath
Calm black wish
Remember pre orange

FIRST LID

Lift yellow off
Forge violet on
Throw blue back

WHAT WHAT

Red pull swing
Push white string
Lull C green

BROUGHT TO MIND

Groove tangerine joy
Thrash ebony perfect
Outside lime nothing

BLENDER BLONDE

Ride on, yellow
Ride on yellow
Red red gold

MUCH AS I'D LIKE TO FORGET

Red quite solemn
Raucous red brief
Bed painted red

BONE

Quest amber tease
Test amber breeze
Anchor azure still

THAT POINT (LIFT)

Rest roost pink
Creep red bare
Crimson hold it

FROM EVERYTHING

Out out red
In blown blue
Now nothing brown

CROWD

Purple nag lilac rag
Shout of silent print
Regal rule red brew

LIFE SWIRL

Orange drop forgot
Rock purple curled
Rest of yellow

WHERE THE HORIZON TAKES YOU

Excuse me you
The nondividing line
Gray white blue

UNTITLED

Black
Gray

Blacker
Grayer

What
White

MERE MORNING

Under spree green
Midst tooled tangerine
Over placid marine

THAT TRIPLET LIFE

Monorhythmic cerise heart
Furnace cerulean burn
Tiny chartreuse churn

SWEPT EDGE

White blue purp
Crossing divine vision
Rage middle thing

STOP HEAR

Ear twist flesh
Over orange o
Pink lift life

VERTALIGN

expansive monochrome
saturaluminous
invertorientation

RUDY

night	soft	black
swim	red	kiss
blood	leaves	leaves

WHATEVER YOU

Say gray
Too blue
Mean green

Urdu Poems

SONG
after Dr. Shafiq

I've left
I got a mortgage
Sold the house didn't repay the mortgage
So marry me
In my last life you said no
This time around—I am rich and on the lam
So let's do it do it do it
Let's invent love
And spin in the opposite
Direction from the world

THE REVOLUTIONARY
after Kamal Hamid

When you're a revolutionary you must
Resolve the riddle of Doing by Doing More

Blood is only liquid
The result is ice

Not to melt
But to hold its form

What was that you said?
Sit still a thousand years

The stars will
Move for you

LOVE POEM
> *after Hammad*

Make an arc with your hand
Put an arrow in that bow
Shoot the arrow into your Lover's heart

Touch the bare ground, the flowers you remember there
Your lover's feet the flowers now, on the dust
Trembling and dancing to the silent songs

Toast with invisible wine, hear the sun in thunder
Sure it's raining. Let your skin be your clothing.
The fiery roses dangle with redness and set the gardens all aglow

THE TALE OF THE TAJ MAHAL
> *after Hassan Abbas Raza*

Be my guest and be my pleasure
May I introduce you to the Taj Mahal?

My name is Shah Jehan—don't laugh!—and
This little bauble is your new home

The name is "Taj Mahal," which translates: "Not Too Shabby"
I see you playing there with your friends, laughing at me

The last moments of life are approaching
Your visit however makes them easy to bear

LOVE

after Salahuddin Nasir

Before there was Something
There was Nothing
Hello Something
Hello you, hello love, hello hello.

There is no simile for Flower
I will wait like a Tiger
I will pounce like a Stone
With no Moth
The Candle burns alone

TRUTH AND CONSEQUENCES
                after Mun Mohan Alam

I speak the Truth
For the first time
So you hear it as lies

This Truth creates a new world
Outfitted with new societies
The old lies are now true!

These new truths create this new world
We live here
Tomorrow when I leave
Rename the world

BODY & SOUL
                after Ashraf Mian

Look!—the Spirit is saying good-bye to the Body!
They leave space so that they each may leave

Skin tears where wings once connected
There is nothing else, and the sky covers it

A cloud—"That is the Body," says the Soul
A cloud—"That is the Soul," says the Body

What tyrant demands this separation?
When we rejoin, our Mind will forget him
It is Body & Soul that will carry the scar

WHO AM I?

after Francis Tanveer

Faithful? Not today.
Faithless? No way.

White? What do you say.
Arab? Look the other way.

Muslim, Hindi, Christiani
Sindhi, Balochi, or Punjabi . . .

I don't believe in Belief.
I believe in What Is.
God told me about this.
God told me about that.
God told me about everything.

That's why I
Am the pie
In God's eye.

SPRING

after Ijaz Bhatti

Watch out—it's spring!
Take your clothes off
And let's do it do it do it

It's spring—make love with love
Hug love and kiss love
Make love with love

The other side—death? suicide?
Away away! I'm busy in love
The molecules are dancing, recombining

I remember you, My Love
Love is you is love
Wow. What happened to words.

All I can say is Love.
Love love love love love
Love love love love love
My mouth is loving love
As it is saying love
I am trying to hold you love

But you are going out there loving
It is spring it is love
Love love love love love

PEACE TREE

after Bashir Khokar

Peace tree
Tree gives peace
Sit in shade. Sleep.
War wakes you up screaming hate
In your ear

Build a frothy mansion
Expensive condo of hate
Or tiny apartment of love?
What you are hiding
Is already showing

Lions have disappeared
Wolves rule the earth
The vultures are everywhere
Birds don't fly anymore
Stumble around drunk with doubt

How can a man be a thief?
Because we all are.
How can a donkey
Be more than an ass?
How can man evolve?

Immediately Poems (Rilke & Kandinsky)

CREAM PUFF EPICENTER

They look so cool in they
Look so cool blue heads and pearls
Babies in the U

ALL-NEW NEUROSIS

You can imagine the opposite
A skinbare sleeping bag in the foyer
The glacial steam begetting time
Eyeball to eyeball
The opposite being not
The opposite containing
The thing itself

The glacier slowly melting
Into treacherous technicolor life

PALACE ALLEY

Big green trees light the way
'Neath four shooting stars
Tears of the moon ripple sea
A frame of wood and beauté

THE OTHER WAY

Locomotive churgs out the century
Electric lights pop speed
But shadows are people
Never get out of the car
Never wear the same white border
The other way from the sun

THE THIRD PHASE

In a basement somewhere
Manger turns over baba
Little childe spills future

First waterfall becomes salad
Then the frame becomes the thing
Now the bundled nerve

Oh her horses race the future
Head on past the past by a nose
Sun shot out of a cannon rock

Driving mouth union
Lifting gently over
Her dress trims the green

PURE EXPRESSION

A black blob way up there
Flies so sweetly by
Let's drop the strings of all pretense
Make our way into the black blob

SACRIFICE

My mother gave birth
To me so I could take
Off my head and hand it to you

ONE CLOWN TO ANOTHER

Around the ring it's fun
A freshly furnished garden
Harmless germoids watch 'em tango dance
You call that a secret?

ONE RED EYE

Blink a room of bad paintings
Turn a circle out of prison
Air raid! Fata Morgana! Winter!
No escape—a little flame everywhere

IN MUNICH POOL HALL

Beer is normal
Toothpicks are brought
Blue cabbage
Spilling water smoke
Layers are liars
To sweet onion heart

BECOMING THE OTHER

Everyone loves you when you're someone else.
—ROBERT STONE

From here from there
The door knocks the air
A patient rises above
The placid table, looks
Below—far below—beneath
The floor to see the sea
The cemetery C
Which is me
And then how over but
All's the same as not
A moment too soon stops
The wild flutter and motors
The censor to approbation
Kicking and screaming
Wave breaks on your fear

K. UND MUNTER AM TISCH

I was hatched without this much troubling coffee
So you paint, why paint me?
So my garters don't show said Wassily
To the teacup set just so

WHAT ACTUALLY HAPPENED

I put on
My bone glove
Androgynous dream
Crept over your body
Bone glove groped
Lips, pulled them out
Froze me with your kissing

SOMEONE JUMPS

Off the horse over the fence
Begins a few poems
Back over the fence onto the horse

IMPRESSION

Impression is what came before, now
Here we go standing by where they were
They now ghost into a view you see
We squint at same red sun
Black outline holding my hand

TOTAL HEART

Improv Japanese science
Zip patches quietly
Content in sheer verb
I'll call my whole life "study"
Venus Awakes

No light
All touch
Funny lines
New tattoo

RHYTHMS, STRONG AND FREE

No shortcut to beauty
First the desire then that
Which fills the desire
Gray spring day in Munich
Gray spring day in Munich

DACHAU

This sadness no bird
Would sing
Grim, gray ground
Stone mud crematorium
Gas chamber
Words spell nowhere else

CONCENTRATION

Every stone
Every bedding
Every breath
Every oven
Every thought
Every one forever

AFTER RILKE

O Rose, O pure contradiction
Enjoy being in no one's sleep
Under so much ice
Barbarous Boring Bullshit

A cuppa jav, a coupla eyes
Dum de dum

The swinging door
Just don't swing
The way it usta
In Glockamorra

THE LOVERS (RILKE)

See how the lovers come into being
Spirit flowing in their arteries
Their bodies tremble like axels
A circle of magnetic heat surrounds them
Thirst, and they become the drink
Wake up and see . . . they become seeing
Let them sink into each other
So that they can overcome

MY ONLY REGRET

That we didn't do Death
That we didn't do breath
Nor use the word nor
Nevertheless it was fun
Chewing gum
Am Starnbergersee

Someone looks at the lake
Someone is on the lake

Someone is in the lake
The lake is slowing the someone
The lake is seeing
The lake is taking

FRANKFURT WHEELS ON

Across the Main
Forsythia blooms ahead
Of spring sudden blue
Remembers tiny iris
Glistening with dew
Beside the scraper

PUBERTY NEUROSIS

O gimme gimme gimme
Gimme do gimme do gimme gimme do
Or else or else or else else else

I wanna wanna wanna
Wanna wanna wanna
You're a creep I just thought you would like to know

Ripping eight years
From your life
Where do they go

Yellow suns on young boy
Tossed into the river
It's a beautiful view
Too bad you cannot see

SMALL FLOWERS OF SOLITUDE ZONE

Mundsburger Brücke

I am falling
Deep
Into the Außenalster
There is no canal
That leads here
You can barely hear
The daffodil creeping up
Through spring
Nature naturally sweeps
The breeze into your lungs
So many of you
Calmly wearing skin inside

A PENDULUM FOR LIFE

Free sun orbit!
Keep mind proceeding somehow out eyes
No sleeping, sleeping
A candle seen through a body
Clicking insects on a blue glass window

LITTLE WHEELS IN AFRICA

The woman is shouting
Her mouth to my eye
I was on top
Of the mountain
Mow the mountain

LATE-NIGHT BULLY

One star wept
It was all all right staring
It was a simpler vocabulary
Made simply of stone

GOD APPEARS IN HUMAN FORM

Put the fish
In the air!
And the mammal
Underground!

ON THE WAY (TO NOWHERE) (NOT HAVING FUN)

While being led
Over the ungraffitied parts
Of the crumbling wall
I bled a kiss

SOMEONE ELSE'S HAIRCUT

In case you were still wondering
Wake up! Escaped birthdays
Have built little pockets where
The trains go, where the sweet
Snow trails the morning
And I don't know doesn't work
Reflecting upon the face in the soup bowl
Most tenderly regret rien

ICE BLITZ

Because you stand alone
In the middle of the room
Trying to balance the world
Life's pendulum shouts escape
As the door opens
To let you back in again

SQUARE ANGEL

Wings fall squarely
Over the statue's face
Not a shame
Just an air conditioner

WALKING MODERN

Steps of angels hidden
Psychopathic remnants of a fool
There was a moment for the true pigeon
All I can say is nothing

And a yellow hat
To tip the sea
From my clanging stupidity

KNEELING BY MY OWN COFFIN

A black blob lifts from the ground
I am amazed at how sweet I
Lie with a sense of casual relief

BECKONING THE WALRUS

Sit in your big silent chair
Pick stuffing from the rip
Without threading the connections
Idly grasp mustache

FISH ON TRAPEZE

Swimming on the mirror is forbidden
No swimming on the mirror!
A cough ends the millennium
Just like that pendulum
Back through the open door again
                    cloud

                              village on the
tree   horizon

            horse

        chaussée
        de plomb

RED CROSS

A circle
Horizon
Light blinks
Stays on

HORSE WITHOUT A TITLE

Bird without a song
Dog without a chase
Roll boxcars boxcars roll

CAVE OF LOVE

How often I hide in
    the cave of love
You on the bed your hand
    dangling
Fingers deliriously glance
    the rug
My skin contorts into
    shape
Your crazy love and the infinite
    space
When the happiness laps upon
    your beautiful truth
And I am lost in this poem
    writing this poem

NO ONE HOLDS A CANDLE

The light itself creates
The waxy surface of the morning wash
A work of light lifts gently
The metaphor to reveal
The clouds unveiling hoop
The sky humming
Itself into being

I CAN'T REMEMBER

When I told you that
Poem it was like a
Dream within a dream—
You were talking I was
The words were coming
Out I was waking up
Over and over and out

ICH WAR DA

Messer im Kopf
Kopf am Tisch
Tisch ist Welt
Wann Kommen Sie?
Besonders warum—
Parken verboten
Über alles

EVERYTHING WITHOUT THINKING

Played Star Club (Hamburg) last night
Waterski Starnbergersee one foot
What's the matter with me? Nothing
A good suicide won't cure

G'night, sweet discontinued currency
I've given the key
To the cat who lies awake
Breathing the ocean
Back to life

ONCE UPON A LIFE

As sweet Death began its lullabye
I was granted as many wishes as I wanted
But it was only my life my life
Passing for my eyes

◆◆◆◆◆◆◆◆◆◆◆◆◆◆◆◆◆◆◆◆◆◆◆◆◆◆◆◆◆

Jeliya!

(OR, GRIOT POEMS, AS SUNG BY PAPA SUSSO

TO BOB HOLMAN)

◆◆◆◆◆◆◆◆◆◆◆◆◆◆◆◆◆◆◆◆◆◆◆◆◆◆◆◆◆

READY?

Not ready to start the story
but how about the song?
Not ready to start the song
but how 'bout float
the river, the boat?
First song sings for
the second and in singing
becomes the story oh
Sing for the second, the Other,
the third with ears, the partner
The moon, the river with ears
moon reflected in water—Listen

I met Professor Bob Holman in Asmara, Eritrea, in the year 2000 when we both participated in a conference, Against all Odds: African Languages and Literatures into the 21st Century. Bob and I hit it off right away, and have been friends ever since. He is part of my family and I am part of his. He has learned the griot and oral tradition (Jaliyaa) from me and I learned the poetry way from him. Bob listened to me sing our epic narratives while I played the kora. I also talked with him in English about Jaliyaa, about Sundiata Keita, the Emperor of the Old Mali empire, and other West African stories and songs and histories. The following poems are based on these songs of kings, queens, and warriors and are inspired by our oral tradition, the griot way.

When we perform together, we follow both traditions. In a way, Bob represents the United States of America to me, and I represent the griot tradition for him. We are friends and brothers, and we have both enjoyed traveling and performing together. Bob also made a movie about griots. It includes me and my son Karamo and many of my family in the Gambia, including my hometown, Sotuma Sere, in the Upper River Region of my country. But I am still waiting for my Hollywood contract!

When Bob asked me to collaborate with him on these poems, we hoped to bring the African oral tradition to educators and students. In my view, education consists of more than the sum of what a man knows, or the skills he can put to his own advantage. Education must improve the soundness of students' judgment of people and things, and their ability to be of service. Bob and I hope that exposure to the griot oral tradition will lead to academic respect for our traditions and culture.

I hope these Mandinka songs that I helped Bob translate into English will introduce many more people to the traditions of my people, and the long history of griot and the Mande-speaking people of the Old Mali Empire. It is not easy to translate an oral tradition in Mandinka to a written tradition in English. But I believe these poems are still alive, and continue to sing even on the page. And I hope you get to hear Bob perform them with me singing and playing kora some day, because it is the combination of science and song that creates the possibility of human happiness and makes life worth living. God bless you!

How Kora Was Born

This story begins long long long long long long long ago
So long ago that it was a place not a time
There was a man
He was so alone
The only person he could talk to was Africa
Luckily there was a tree nearby
Even more luckily behind that tree
That is where his partner was hiding
All the sun and all the water were condensed
Into a single tiny block
Which the man planted in the sandy soil
He blew and he blew on that spot
Each time he blew he thought he heard something
What he was hearing was of course his partner singing
The man did not even know what singing was
Because he could only talk
He could not sing yet
So he blew and he listened, blew listened blew listened
And the plant pushed out dark green
And began to twist and grow
A vine reaching for the breath
And stretching toward the song
(Because it was made from sun and rain, remember?)
So at the end of the vine that was the calabash
And the tree it was not a tree anymore
It was the neck and handles
That was when the man's partner, Saba Kidane
Came out into the open (but that's another story)

57

And the breath and the singing and the vine?
Well, there are twenty-one strings, what do you think?
And now you say what about the bridge and the cowhide
And the rings that tie the strings to the neck
So you can tune the kora?
Hey, what about the thumbtacks that hold
The cowhide taut over the calabash
And the resonator hole?
Well you go right on talking about all that
I am playing kora now
Next time I'll tell you about the cow

Jeliya!

Yay! Jaliyaa!
Alaleka Jaliyaa Daa!

God created the art of music
This music! This song!
This song is a celebration!
A celebration for the griots! For the jeli!
Whenever griots perform a ceremony
We will perform this song of praise
To honor and commemorate all the griots and griottes
Not just one! All of us! The many many many voices
The griots as part of West African society
Mandinka, Bambara, Fulani, Wolof, Sarahule
Just to name a few
        These are the voices
                That carry the tradition

Yay! Jaliyaa!
Alaleka Jaliyaa Daa!

Hey, Horseriders!
How brave you are!
To face the enemies
I mean the enemies of Peace
Enemies of Peace-loving people
Tighten your belts! Fight hard!
So that peace will remain on the earth

Yay! Jaliyaa!
Alaleka Jaliyaa Daa!

Jelimusso and Jelikaylu!
All female griottes, all male griots!
Hold strong to the tradition
The practice brought to you
A gift from your ancestors
Passed down voice by voice
From generation to generation
It's a long and glorious tradition
That we must always try to keep
Because this is who we are
We know who we are
Because we know where we came from
That is the meaning of History
That is the meaning of Poetry
This is the song of Jeliya

Yay! Jaliyaa!
Alaleka Jaliyaa Daa!

Yay! Jaliyaa!
Alaleka Jaliyaa Daa!

Kaira Peace

Kaira is a word
It is the word for Peace
Kaira means Peace—I think you can hear that
Kaira! Oh how Papa Susso loves that word! Kaira!
Papa Susso, the internet griot with a BA degree
It is such pleasure to sing Kaira up and down kora strings
Listen to Kaira, that pleases Peace, Please Peace Now
Slavery is over, that's what Peace means
1945, West Africa, you know the World War
Was happening—Kaira!—but in West Africa,
In Senegambia, 1945 was the year slavery was abolished
No more slaves means Peace—Kaira!
Now it so happened that a few years later
There was a rich man in Guinea
Name of Kaira-ba Toure, his name
Was Peace and he loved Peace so it was all together
And there was a great great great balafon player, I'm talking
Teneng Sory Diabate, who saw this and rededicated Kaira
To this patron of the arts and this patron of Peace, Kaira, Kaira-ba

Now listen: Here is Kaira

Slavery abolished but people still fight for power, Kaira
The jeli sing Kaira and people who come from the slave families,
Well, they still call themselves slaves, they walk around
Only now they follow no one. They are looking for work
    like everyone else.
And the power struggles you could say they go on to this day

This New Year's Day, let's know this word—Kaira!
It's a word for Peace, it pleases Peace, Please Peace Now
With slaves in Mauritania and Sudan—Kaira
With political prisoners in the u.s. and Eritrea—Kaira
With people dying in Iraq even though the war is not a war—Kaira
The kora plays the contradictions and plays for Kaira, for Peace
That is Kaira, the word for Peace
Please Peace Now
Kaira is the word for Peace

Allah L'a Ke

Allah L'a Ke means "It is God's will"

This is the story about a king and two of his sons
His name is Fallai Kora of Tambasansang in the eastern part
    of the Gambia
He was king for so long long a time
These were the days when a king would die, you don't vote,
No way! It was the oldest son who would take over

So now this king has two sons from two different mothers
Traditionally these two boys would always have rivalry
This is fadinyah—same-father-different-mother-rivalry

Now after some time the prince (always the oldest son)
Named Mamadi Kora traveled, oh, a week or so
And this was when the king got sick
And died.

This is a story from the 16th century!
This is the century when the colonial masters came to West Africa,
When the British took the river and claimed the Gambia for
    Britain and
This was when a District Commissioner was in charge of the
    whole administrative office in the area.
He is called "Britain" too—sing coincidence!
Kora plays coincidences . . . .

The District Commissioner Britain came to the village of
    Tambasansang to appoint a new king.

So he arrives, he says, Who is the successor? Who is next of kin?
So the town answers, Oh, yes, ahem, right, well,
Kemonding Kora, that would be the one!
Now, this was the prince's younger brother
Why did they do that? Well, I am coming to that.

They did that because Mamadi Kora was a bad bad person
And therefore nobody liked him in the community.
What did he do that was bad? Wait, I am coming to that.

So
The District Commissioner appointed Kemonding and left.
Good-bye Good-bye. . . .

But when Mamadi Kora came back from his journey
He said WHAT? He said WHY? And the villagers answered,
Umm, yes, well, the European man came and he just decided.

Well instead of the District Commissioner Britain, Mamadi
    just went to a
Marabout man to make a juju to change things back around

Now the juju man took a cutlass and put some writings on it—
    it was Mandinka in Arabic—
And said to Mamadi, OK you take this cutlass to your brother
And as soon as he sees these writings that will be the end of his era
And the Marabout man said, Make sure this meeting is just
    the two of you
So the best time to do this would be, oh . . .

So
At three in the morning Mamadi came to Kemonding's door
Knock knock I want to talk to you
But instead of just showing the writing, Mamadi raised the
    cutlass up—
And guess what! Of course!

Kemonding screamed in fear for his life, waking up everybody
    who came rushing in
And they arrested Mamadi and threw him in jail and contacted
District Commissioner Britain that there was
A threat to the life of the new King!

The next day the Commissioner came to the village:
Bring this man out! I must interview him.

Why you want to kill the King?
Noooooooooooooooooooooooooooooo! I don't want to kill
    the king! This man is my brother and I just wanted to
    show him the words on the blade!
When you came here before, you did not realize I was the
    next of kin!
It is I who am the rightful King!

No one spoke.
Then one of the griots, Kunkung Kanuteh, stood and talked and
    played the kora, and sang.
Here is his poem:
Mr. Commissioner I want you to hear me
What this man says is right enough, he was King Fallai Kora's
    eldest son

But O! Mr. DC, What a bad man he is
He is greedy. He is not generous. He is a White Man—whoops,
Good thing
You do not understand Mandinke,

Let's just leave it in English,

Mamadi is a bad man!

I hear you, said the DC, but I also hear the traditions speaking.
I must obey the Gambian traditions, I cannot change them—
I respect them so now I must appoint Mamadi the new King!

OK but
Just then the juju started to work.
I don't need to tell you what happened next
Kemonding ruled a long long long long long long time and
     everybody loved him
And I don't know what happened to Mamadi
The DC just disappeared
And as for juju, and traditions, I do know a good Marabout you
     can go to.

Kulafaso! Celebration for the Feast of Feasts

Folks, guess what? It's Celebration Time!
Kulafaso! Kulafaso!
The whole village is celebrating
We've come together so let's celebrate
How can we celebrate New Year's?
I got a good idea
I got it from the griot, Papa Susso
(What a voice he has!)
(Also not a bad kora player)
Let's go visit Jojo Diggery, aka Jekere Bayo
Why shall we do that? you may ask
Let's ask Papa—Papa, why visit Mister Jekere Bayo?
Only one reason, Bob—he is the richest man in the village
And once he hears our poem about New Year's
He'll shower us with positivity in the form of cash
With which we can fuel the celebration
And make everyone happier and more joyous
And prosperous to the extreme in the New Year
We'll dedicate this to all the businessmen
So that Jekere Bayo won't feel like he's the only patron
We can do this poem at the Bowery Poetry Club
And we can record this song and all our fans can shower
Us with their greenery, their fine dances and great jokes

We know how to celebrate!
Kulafaso! Kulafaso!
Without the poem there can be no celebration
Without the poem there can be no New Year!

Happy New Year to the whole village from Papa & Bob
This message was brought to you by Jekere Bayo

Kumbija Kantaba

A funny one
a person with very very bad luck
God hates him!
that's what Kumbija Kantaba means
to the extent that whatever he does,
there's God, shaking his head
and wondering why he isn't doing something else

Even when he was a baby, his clothes didn't fit
then they tried some old worn-out clothes—why,
they'd lift him up and try them on and they fit good
so rags, it was decided, would be his wardrobe

Leftovers were all he craved
he was a loser at school, lessons
didn't stay in his head, his teachers
nicknamed him
Kumbija "Frustration" Kantaba

He tried to get a job then
and you know what, he couldn't even
get an interview, that's right

He's a very hard-working man
but no luck at all
say he goes to a big feast—well,
his food turns to mud or sand
while the other people's food is gooood, so good

69

Tubanyou—maize, Delicious!
sanyo—millet, Incredibly tasty!
mano—rice, Wow!
even geo—water, thirst-quenching water
geo—turns to blood
ooooooooooooooooh

So one day he goes
and sits under a big jahlo tree

"God!" he cries to the skies
"God!
I did everything! I tried everything I could
but no success
I have never enjoyed anything!
God! So please go ahead and kill me!"
Then a big branch falls off the tree and lands right beside him
the man jumps up and runs off shouting
"Now I understand everything!"

The Loving Father's Song

Papa Susso's Poem for His Young Children
Moussa, Kinda, Fatoumata, Sarjo, Abdullah

The first time a father tells his child
The child is nowhere to be seen

The second time
What is that strange buzzing I hear

The third time the child
Must go get something to eat

And then on the fourth time
The child starts to hear something

When I tell you it the fifth time
You say to me, Are you talking to me

And on the sixth time you reply,
What language is that you are speaking

By the time I have told you the seventh time
The words become a song and the poem becomes the kora

And you must learn it my little griots
And then you can repeat the story

And the story goes like this:

Forty-eight years I have been working,
Spreading the word of the griot
Spreading the word around the world
And sending the money home to you

And Sankung is here
And Al Hassan is here
And Fatou is on her way
And Mariama is on her way
And Karamo is on his way

And I think I may be on my way
On my way back to the Gambia
To return to the griot life at the Koriya Musa Center
      for Research in Oral Tradition at Sotuma Sere

So my dear children
Who carry the word of the griot
From my father Alhaji Bunka Susso, jelikuntigi of the Gambia
Through me to you and back to the first Susso who made
      the first kora
I sing the song of the father who tells the children it is time
      for them to begin
The new generation of which I sing
And which you will live and carry on
And buy each others' tickets and pay for each others' rent
And teach each other the ways of Africa and the United States
Of Gambia and the world
And know this song is the loving father's Father Song

Manjugulong!

Poem to Provoke the Appearance of Saba Kidane

Manjugulong!
Manyinijugalong!
Bayayaylaylanna!

(I don't know who is my enemy
I don't know who is my friend
Everyone is laughing at me!)

Once long long long long well actually not so long ago
In Asmara we were sitting around as we are now sitting
    around
    here and
!Saba Kidane!

She was something else!
Which means she was something
Her absence makes her presence felt
O Saba! We sing to provoke your appearance

Maybe—we should just move New York to Asmara?
Maybe—we should all speak one language?
Call it Poetrysabakidane?

If only you were a forty-year-old family man with a real job!
Instead of the great young poet you are—we hear your poems
    today, Saba
Yes, because you are young, and a woman, they say you will not
    come back

To Asmara, to your two children—they say, if only you were
    a forty-year-old man!
O Saba! We sing to provoke your appearance

Manjugulong!
Manyinijugalong!
Bayayyaylaylanna!

(I don't know who is my enemy
I don't know who is my friend
Everyone is laughing at me!)

O Saba surely did like the way that Papa played the kora
She said those strings had magic power—Super Power!
Now we know what "Super Power" means
It's what it takes to keep a poet from her job
To continue to keep US apart from Africa's heart
O Saba! We sing to provoke your appearance
Manjugulong!

So Lo Lay

Come close, closer, So Lo Lay, my child.
Listen close and closer.
Let my body be the words you understand
Let the sound of the kora strings be the words
Let the words live, the beat
Of the music, the beat
Of our hearts, come listen close, come closer

o.k., here's the song first sung to the little boy So Lo Lay
I'm the parent, you're the child
We're each other, but I have something to say
Education is not in the dusty school down the road
Education is right here in my heart, in this song
What is good and what is bad? Here.
   Let me tell you, sing you
   Let kora tell and sing

So Lo Lay, So Lo Lay
So Lo Lay, So Lo Lay

And what happens if I haven't told you something
And you do something bad? Why, that's o.k.
That once. But after I tell you, then you must learn
What's the right thing to do, the good thing, So Lo Lay,
And learn about the bad things, the things not to do, too,
   So Lo Lay.
And if you do those bad things, after you've learned
   right/wrong,

Then you will apologize. Nobody's perfect!
And then you'll never do them again. Because you have heard
The song, So Lo Lay, you have learned the song.
And you will remember, you will remember this song,
    So Lo Lay,
You will know and you will remember
And you will sing this song, So Lo Lay.
Sing this song now, with me, come close, closer, So Lo Lay . . .

Mokoiro—for Haiti

"To Help"

Old song, "To Help," it is human
Sometimes nothing happens, then
Something happens and you need to have something else happen
Haiti, I will sing for you
Mokoiro, to help, to help Haiti

A line comes to your house
Earthquake, line of people
Line of earth and water and line of people, too
Let all of us help Haiti
The catastrophe is all of ours
The children need help, Mokoiro, you can hear them

The kora is crying
Because people are crying
And the kora is the people, you know that
When tragedy comes it's our duty to help
This is what makes us human
And that's what gives us the beauty of the kora

Sad news streams from my fingers
Tears are in my voice
This is the song "Mokoiro," help Haiti
And I will sing the song with all of your help
Your Mokoiro, your gift to Haiti

Your help is like a song from the kora
Because when something happens, a tragedy—
Then something else happens, we will help.
Mokoiro! We will help Haiti! Help Haiti now!
Listen to the song "Mokoiro" and help Haiti now!

Tara

Sheikh Omar Futiyou Taal! Sheikh Omar Taal!
Sheikh Omar Taal! A religious fourteenth-century Malian man
Tara means "He is gone"
Moussa yea yea!—La la la

when papa growls
the earth shakes and
is in transformation
from voice to earth

deep goes the voice
deep goes the earth

when kora strings soar
then voice sings and zips along
like a kite string without a kite
what is holding up the string?
that is the wind of the wind
the wind, you see, has a secret that only
the jeli can tell you
just as sound has meaning
so the wind has other wind we call tara

the strings are sailing along lightly
they are flying (no kite to
hold them up, as I said before)

and then
along comes the kora
to snap the string
put them in verse
like a beautiful dress, *dondinko*
the Manding word for dress

he came from a place called Ségou
a city well known around the world
Walliou—God-sent messengers
God sent many many many many Walliou
to deliver messages to all the people
wonderful things to open people's eyes

before Sheikh Omar Taal was born his father had a dream
that he was going to have a son like that
there was an older brother, one year two months old
his father was a Marabout, they were traveling by foot step by step
    by step by step
it gets dark and it is time for prayer
Hayred, the Fourth Prayer, evening prayer
Sheikh Omar's father says, "We have to pray"

his wife put the baby down and they started to pray
a hyena came and came closer, closer, threatening them
but his father and his mother were praying to God
they could see Allah so they did nothing
the hyena took the baby away
Sheikh Omar's father says "Wife! Why didn't you save the baby? I
was praying to God"
his wife said, "You serve only one person, I serve two—God and you

as you are my husband, I cannot stop
if you had stopped, I would have stopped—but I cannot, alone"

"o.k. if that is the reason why you couldn't stop
I am going to ask Allah to give you a new baby
and this baby will be known all over the world
for the sacrifice that his mother made to Allah"

"Oh great Allah," cried Sheikh Omar's father,
"you have seen what has happened with the hyena and my baby"
Allah replied, "I'm going to give you a Walliou child,
born in Segou, a very famous town"

at fifteen, Sheikh Omar witnesses a great Walliou prosperity
and is asked to be the chief, the king—"No" he replies
"I cannot because as chief I cannot serve God in the proper way
I want to be Allahkajong—a servant of God"

next thing you know Sheikh Omar fights a holy war for God
it's a long long long long long story
it could take all day. it's all about how Islam came to that part
    of Africa
it's about the Christian missionaries and their battles to control
    Africa
it's about the animists and their desire to keep the old ways
and its all about the Walliou, the messenger who brought the
    songs of Allah
the songs for the griots
Sheikh Omar moved from Segou to Hamdallah
then a griot came from another town to Segou but didn't know
that Sheikh Omar had gone. Instead he sees the churches that

the missionaries have built
he sees the European schools
he picks up his ngoni and begins this song
"Tara!" he begins, "Sheikh Omar Taal is gone!
Tara! He is gone!"

Memory Made Real

(OR, YOU ARE NO LONGER HERE TO WASH YOUR HAIR)

. . . love it. Lights on eyes open now close round moment called First Kiss and then. And now lights off eyes open as we are to each other now forever can't count years children poems paintings. Forever as we know and only we know is now, eternal now knowing/not knowing. Hold you laugh with you world has served us up to each other, luscious, physical, and gentle, Venus from sea. Two days is forever now if we can hold the moment as you hold me I hold you. That's all I ask for everything. And a simple moment. And everything else a memory

Forget Yesterday

What never happens,
Happens. The green bow.
Mercies. A light rain. Mother
And stepfather, the job of it. If I
Could do it all over, the pushing
Briefly set aside, dusty life.

The weary world's born all over;
The jungle rots into sensuous
Lubricity. A clear path is laid out
Behind you, and to go that way
Is to disappear forever. Because

It's the past. It's the past that never
Was. It's the unwilling will be. Come
On baby now, let's go surfing now
Come on a surfin' safari with me.

Born Orphaned

—for Elizabeth

I

I was
A wanderer
I answered
The phone

"You have come
here to die"
Not quickly
Eventually

YOU

A home is not
Something you can buy
A love
Cannot
Be spoken
Here with you, singing
I write this poem

THE SHAPE

We moved through seasons
Like fish
And we moved through the years
Like a gravel riverbed

CLOUDS

You must close your eyes
    to listen
Your skin tells
    everything

MOUNTAIN

We were in the Midwest
Looking for mountains
The wind couldn't go around
And there were no shadows
We called it "bed"

LAST NIGHT

A rain tonight, light on
    the screen
I turn to see you
Looking at me
A night remembered
Like a place
Indelibly marked
On a map
Of us

ANOTHER

Sweet day
On the planet
Knowing you
Are on it

WE

We went swimming the other day and forgot to surface

THRILL

When I open the window
The world rushes in
But I am already gone
I am not there
The world looks all over
But always forgets
Behind the door

MOTIONLESSNESS IN MOTION

Brought together
By chance and rigor
The poem and
The hand

WHAT LOVE IS

I put out my hand
Your face is there

EARS SOUND GOOD

When day reaches tip point's slight hesitation
Thin take of breath, settling agitation
And the moors' mossy bog birch sheds tarty tear
The thought rises a whalespout—I wish I had me an ear

ON THE EDGE OF THE OLD LAGOON

Our boat, our boat
Nestling into the lagoon
Your lips
Nestling into my neck

ALMOST PERFECT GESTURE

Here at the airport connections
        and farewells
But we live here! These tides
        Our easy breaths

BACK TO BACK IN THE DAY

When I think of how you
Were before I knew you
I can't imagine
Such a world

DEAREST SWEET DREAM COME REAL,
WHERE BREATHING IS KISSING

Now I smell like your hands are on me, holding my face
My eyes liquid and wash ashore in your eyes
Your body my body the ocean become
Riding time till we vanish and here you are

TIE MY SHOES

I bow and bend
to tie
    my shoes
May I tie yours
together
    with mine

DIGITAL CLOUDS

How often I stop and realize I haven't stopped
And come to myself again as a stranger named Walt

SIGNATURE OF ALL THINGS

Under your eyelid
The poem never sleeps

EFFORTLESSLY HUMAN

Crossing the street
I cannot do it
I turn in the middle of traffic
And come home to you

LITTLE AFRICA

If I were young now I'd be in Africa
I've been there three times
You've never been there
We tend the garden and we wait for rain
Dry as it is here
On the edge
Of the Sahara

EVERYWHERE IN PARTICULAR

How did we end up here
In this place, in this bed,
In this sky, in this tomb,
In this shoe, in this kiss
I don't care it's everywhere
Being here with you

We Met in Managua

It was 1988 and everybody was young and skinny
sang marched and picked coffee
And drank beer and rum and slept on the floor and
Married each other barefoot
people diving smooth surfaces
into rocky interiors discover
Meditation is not meditative! It is rocky.

Also making love
is not such smooth sailing either, contains a passionate bite.
Ah well, let me go meditate!

A Day

This is a day for a walk
To walk me by the river
To find an outdoor laundromat
And do our clothes
To have some cereals, different
Ones, with yogurt, fruited,
Some juice, strong black cafe

To walk talking of nothing
To watch our feet conversing
Children yawning, the wind
At a cafe an omelet
Remembering cigarettes

As the sun slowly goes down
Our hands find each other
Sex is stirring, but distant yet
The nudges of breath and eyes
When you are shy I like it
The way night is suddenly here
And we walk home to continue

One Night City Light

Tender morning, diesel Gauloise
Thick hint of impossibility
Sweetly leaning from behind into
The sun running the risk
All paper blinds, slicing the siren
Into even shadows!

Who is looking?
The blue becomes the work, the street
Curves back into a new name. I will
Never leave you, you are never the same.
Kept in a blank book, the reassurance
Of everything, settling down to rise.

It is night. Simple light,
Cat on a line. Your ear nestles
A walnut seashell. Fragrant
Anticipation, next to next.
I am an elevator to whatever
Floor you want to go to, say
"Build," and I scrape the sky
Apart with your tongue's
Eye. Crazy little
We know about the recesses
Of the body goes this
Way that, blood moves round
Room to room. I walk out to
Meet you and when we

Turn into one is there room
Enough for every memory
We insist on putting there? Your
Tears or mine, who's dry first cries.
I know. I know nothing. Put
You first in front of me, on top
Of me, all round me. Surround a whisper
Of your lip, a ship atop a bridge.
Who would put water in the riverbed?
All the beds, you here on my shoulder,
I hear on yours. There. A star
By any other sun. Hush, love comes.

My Parents

There were three
of them
Mom Dad Dad

They were young, they
Didn't raise me

The one I knew the least
Did the most

It makes me think of love
I'm from Ohio

Once I told my mother
You married him (my

Stepfather) for his money!
I'd take it back, she who did the
most could never leave nor protect
Cut! Rewind! Where
do the parents end I begin
Mother was the baritone sax player
in the Harlan (KY) Green Dragon
Marching Band they had to put the
horn on a little trolley it was as tall

as she was five-foot-two Sally Ruth
Lewis Geller Holman Schoenbachler

married the only Jew in town as
has been well documented I was

born Geller adopted Holman:
To My Parents
where would I be without you
space
blowing my brain through a flute

standing on my head do I think
at my age it is right my beard
turning white seeing you
through myself
with my daughters I want

must write great Italian Mama
poem, the Nuyorican Mamacita
Jewishe Mama, Mornbread Mamaw
Daddy
where have you gone all daddies
washed to sea good-bye good-bye
my mother doesn't live in a trailer

but she does live in Florida
married to a good man finally
who treats her right relates to me
as all my fathers with distance
and a lack of approval I will raise
myself from the lack of it hello

I will say to myself
hello hello to the parents
who will ever never know

The Opening of the Big Museum

It was big, you were lost, the art leads you sure, but you are lost
      In the art
There were colors, all friends & shades, & escalators, saying see
      You later
At the top, there is so much space, blink your eyes reopen, leap
      Into space
Remarkably attenuated, yet forcefully blank, there was nothing
    you could do
                      About it
Many's the time you were forced to draw the blinds behind &
    stare solely
           At the art
Wandering drifts so many mazed passages & treats of eye flash
    that you'd stop
           At nothing
Just to see everything was the trick of the day, carousing conflicts
    of mind &
        Memory
At just the right moment the helicopter would land offering to
    whisk you up
                           & away
You wave it on over the edge's horizon and keep on searching for
    what is right
          Before you
The museum is opening, continually opening, waves opening
    you, waves
        Opening you

Florida

Clouds of anywhere
Only Florida all surround
Big toe of pleasure, tiny
Ringlets of multicolor droplets
Mix delightful Day-Glo Shango
Clobber strict sense with heat
A word dissolves on your nipple
Flowing sensate, this cool memory locks
An eternal kiss all over your body
Sweet raucous sashay raw song
Woman man song, the lap of ocean
Into ocean, skin into skin
Into into into
Clouds of anywhere everywhere
Pink dawn over blue

4E59.5

Stop in the name of love! The Supremes, baby—
It's 8:30 a.m. and I'm launching from bed, E. 13th

& the next record is Funky 4 + 1 you could set
Your alarm clock by me stereo having made vow

Always Rock in the Morning my shrink convinces
Me to have my girlfriend not move in we spend

Sixty nights in a row sleeping in each other's arms six months
Together then Libby dumps me and the next night

Turned away airport gate trying for free flight to Europe
("My boyfriend is from Holland . . . Michigan") she runs

Into the ocean doesn't stop in the name of ocean but survives
& schizophrenic that's not right I'll change it as tragic train

Why? Am? I? Here? flowers to bring in every morning walk
The dog, and, on my way home, buy flowers. Put the paper

In the elevator for my wife to bring up, and it's just spring
So today daffodils and daisies for my Daisy. The connection

As Jack Gelber would say, or Einstein and Tu Fu, is: Happy
Birthday, Elizabeth. You are fifty-nine-and-a-half today and
     officially

Retired. Instead we will buy 308–310 Bowery and build
A poetry club. Go for it, in the name of love.

Washing Your Hair

Here it is late as usual
Alone and desiring
Where are you is you are not
Here to wash your hair desiring
Late, alone, with everything
Changing slowly under stem
A little distance like a foot—
Metaphors grow here. Sew
On a button using your hair.

Distortion is distinction,
Lachrymosity slides tender shoot
No weight in your physicality
Anyway. And I can wait.

The Word *Mystery*

Many say the smell is overpowering
but their nasal insecurities are not sufficient
to keep me from setting up basecamp in your armpit

Dewsweat, coalfire, beaverfat, marshmallow,
cross-stitch sampler "Home Sweet Armpit"

I'm reading Ogotomeli, feet up on orange crate,
your face on label
I'd never seen it there before! how'd it get there?
the way you superglue

Photobooth minisnap over author's photo (not Ogotomeli)
it wasn't there! till I 1) finished book 2) put it down 3) sighed
like reading completion good meal—you!

The book, the sampler, the conversation with Ogotomelli
I had and you were with me
looking at me from places you aren't
always me astonishes

How everywhere you are! It's a mystery, a word I never
use because language itself

(Words I mean) are the answer to all mystery. In
    other words, how can it be a mystery if it is
    the word *mystery*, there's no mystery 'bout that!

Just as there is no answer to "answer" in answer.
When I ask the question about the Yummo

The twin prebeings (Andamboulou) of the Dogon
I need to know all this because air

Is water when you are prebeing which sounds O.K.
    but instead of legs
Serpent tails O.K. O.K. It is like looking right
    through you to see the world because
    you are not here and that is the mystery
    of love not to be solved nor answered
    or at least I hope not

View from armpit quite pleasant
smoke from coalfire curling as hairs do

I am dream and driven totally crrazy with the smell
smell deep covering all the complete interior decoration
find world's softest skin rough nest for tongue and sleep

Love

—FOR ELIZABETH

Your hand throws out
As you sleep

And brushes
Another body

Lands and settles
On the other body

Except it is your hand
And it is my body

In Passing

Mention quickly a lung (one
only) that holds air for entire
planet, well! When the elevator
decides on its own how
many floors, there you go. For
kissing complaints, stand
over here, in the Sadness Line.

When she passed from life, I
remember that last kiss. And
following was a moment boats
appearing on dry land. They were
Rescue Boats, making headway
against the wind. Just hold on
a bit longer. Just hold on to me.

To Lisanne

(Birth of First Grandchild)

You are feeding Ant'ny
I am in the office backdoors
The sun is engaging smoothly
Our family's loving attendance

Nurture mush cooliness fills
Your home see Ko-man conquer
The family shuffle deck schedule
Like a pro, you pro, Ant'ny grows

A moment of clarity thanks you
A particle of time bounding fro
Interconnecting life simply at
The nipple & feeding this back to you

Whatever you say will do
Singing this back to you

What Death Means

Something different
For everyone

What Next

Waiting here
Forever

Please Don't Die Yet

On the back
    of the cereal box
It says To Be Continued

The cat jumps
    up on the breakfast table
The crooked painting beckons
Like your next lover

Lightbulb pops
    toaster crackles
        phone just won't shut up
All over there is everything

While here sit you still
As the hole
    in the metal eyepatch
Doctors wear elastic bands
Round their foreheads

When I was five, I made Mom promise
To put a teeny tiny headstone on my grave
The easier to push it off
    and come back to you

Movie Theater Alone You

May I sit in the middle of the row of your body
There is no middle nor end
But the light through plastic that keeps beginning
Boxcar popcorn, the doctor's illicit fatale streams
The giant eyebrow—air or water?
Put your arm around time's fountain, sitting
With your eyeball galloping all over the place
Propelling jolt into space, what once was Space
Suddenly defunded the Space Program. Many stars.
Good thing to do for the rest which is deep
Relaxation exploration of your life. Oh dear
Oh read oh dear oh read
I am off to the races
Where the horses ride the humans
Hold it right there by a noise the end flap flap flap flap

Time Is a Number

That doesn't mean anything, she said, as the years ticked
by too busy to count meaningless count consumption activates
neurotransmitter dopamine depression rising inferring
To the limit to preserve slim chance to shoot through happiness
and come out the other side happiness behind us the frenzy
we've adopted in search of what we hope is happiness and
perfection is in fact a distraction mania a distraction happiness
distraction experience what matters not intellectual expectations
Again sing Happy! Raise your cups, Letters of daughters to fathers

My Children Are My Poems

Last tomorrow moon
A flimsy song's cardboard
Spine spires, no wheel
Can't get to the begin
Can't even end even

Poem for My Daughters in the New Year

Diving straight down at our red chimney
The green is powering up at me

Electric lines give off blue sparks
The clouds are layers of white-and-pink sharks

I see the City like Oz over my wing
What can I give you now, anything?

Sophie, you are twelve and making up a world brashly
Daisy, you are nine and dreaming in an envelope cozily

I have a poem for each of you, with love and your name
Because to me they mean the same

In Daisy's Kitchen, Moose Underfoot

Mike calls to confirm the cake pan. It's Sophie's graduation supper in
 Oakland

And she's prepping for an audition in Berkeley. Three hours ago we
 were Ceremony Itself, on the Main Stage in a Shavian garden,
 same site where fourteen graduates

Just qualified for their Equity cards, the event highly theatrical, totally
 devoid

Of Pomp & Circumstance sap, words words words: the Theatre makes
 its own Music. Willie Brown, Flamboyant San Francisco politico,
 snags an honorary MFA in Acting—Makes hay and jokes. Stu
 and Rory will be here soon, Sascha joining Moose

A party spirit settles in, the idea of home pervades, Susan and RT
 arrive, all hell

Breaks loose, not really. It's a Tuesday feels like Sunday. The chickens
 go in

As the cake comes out. Always use the recipe from the Hershey cocoa,
 Elizabeth says,

And the roasting vegetables smell like earth. Sophie is radiant, Daisy is
 aglow, friendship

Is in the pot, forty years old. Let us leave these partiers as Pete shows
 up with a million

Bucks and Molissa with a refrigerator full of surprise, and slide into the
 fog. Another new day just over the Bridge of Gold. Don't try to
 remember. The story's still being told.

Day for Sophie and Nick, Epithalamium

Maybe it's time, maybe the memory of time,
Maybe the blindness we feel in a world full of strangers,
Maybe a prayer, maybe a memory of prayer,
Maybe a life by the side of the road

If I were to remember how could I forget
All the time what you mean to me
I'd write you a letter. I'd better watch out—
I'm falling. A bottle of you!

The sky is a bed and you live in my head
And I can't stop the kiss that you started
And the thing that Ouija said, as the waiter turned red
Keeps me company just like it started

The heart! Oh the heart of the day!
The way that your lips sealed the poem
If ever I die I'll call out for you
And your answer will be what keeps me living!

Maybe it's time, maybe the memory of time,
Maybe the blindness we feel in a world full of strangers,

My Heart Is a Real Thing

Despite the imprecations of your parents, friends, former
          lovers, teachers, professional crises managers,
               pets, & now you say God Himself/Herself
I would still like to reply via my own tiny but honest opinion
My heart is a real thing
It is & remains untouched by the concerned backstabbings
          of these privileged naysayers
I am yours
A simple gift all of me
My life, such as it is, you decide,
With you, complete. You will be loved.

               You will be loved
In such a way that the streets will rise up to greet you
The rivers will float you across
And the sky itself will also be a means of transportation
The radar screen contains many blips
But only one is steady and equidistant from you
My fair one, my ravishing delight, my True Other
The light touch of your hair on my arm
The slight rustle of breeze is mutual desire

Engage me with your tongue!
Sit here—eat music!
Collaborative sex & our reciprocal love absolute
Love That Has No Other Name is your name
& as I lie back on my bed all I can do

Is sing out for you, in language primal, lost
Singing this language only we understand
Where the No's of the world become our Yes
And Yes is our child,
        Child that is our Love,
                Love That Has No Other Name

Midsummer Kupala

Mirabile Dictu!
Miracle of miracles!
World's Longest Night
Coincides With
World's Shortest Day
Apex of Curvature
Slow Fluttering Midnight of Desire
A dream kindly vision—remarkably elastic tenacity
Clouds gray and blue submerge to silver slivers
So many doors

As the evening rolls into
Who do you love
Except love
There is light in the song
And there is song
In the start
It never ends
Never grows

As remarkable as any one night
The edge hinge of summer

Oh special day oh special night
The Night of Flame
Night of Flower
Oh where have you gone?

Oh everybody where have you gone?

Nothing can bring you back
Here I stand

Slowly the sun gives up the
Lowly the moon rises achingly slowly

When day suddenly appears

So gently gently coming true

Sing This One Back to Me

Honeybee honeybee deep in the honeytree
Do not tell me to suck dry the tips of whip grass
Swan sway swan sway Ganges flows all day
Would you send me off then to the blasting seas?
Tale singer nightingale crooner carousing on the leaf drip
Who dares say, Excuse me, quiet please, eat dry leaf clippings
This robin-rocking tail lit by the fullest moon
Try to redirect to fogbound swirl, see what happens to you
My feet on the lotus? No, my feet are the lotus!
All God? Gosh, I was looking over at you—shh.
No need this talking, this poem so obvious, shh.

Notes

"Fuck Off, I'm a Fuckin' Welsh Fuckin' Learner! (That's the Title)" / "Ffwciwch Oma, Dwin Ffwcin' Dysgwr Ffwcin' Gymraeg! (Dyna'r teitl)": Written, in Welsh, for the Stomp (Y Stomp), the individual poetry slam of the Welsh National Cultural Fair, the Eisteddfod. All poems have to be in the Welsh language—only twelve poets are invited. I was invited because I was, indeed, a Welsh learner. For starters, I'd taken a two-week intensive at the magical Welsh Heritage Center, Nant Gwrtheyrn; shout-outs to Sian Melangell Dafydd, who told me to go there; Llinos Griffith, my super teacher; Grahame Davies, dear friend and co-po, who visited me and ferried me about; and Elinor Robson of the Literature Wales, who believed in my poetry—and my Welsh!

I came back to Wales a few months later (my Welsh teacher in the U.S. was Cynthia Davies, suggested by Catrin Brace—hwyl!) to shoot *Language Matters,* the PBS documentary I'm working on with ace producer-director David Grubin—Welsh is the only language to have been on the official Endangered List and then come off. I arrived a few weeks early, eased into life in Blaenau Ffestiniog (where Welsh is what's spoken), took daily lessons in Welsh Culture from poet/pal Dewi Prysor and family (Rhian, Owain, Rhodri, a Gethin), studied with Delyth Tuffrey, and recorded with musician Gai Toms. More lessons with Sian Teifi, Ifor ap Glyn, diolch yn fawr iawn!

I wrote/pieced together my poem using all the wily poetry slam techniques I'd gathered since starting the Nuyorican Poets Cafe slams in 1989. Such as, always begin with an audience-grabber—in this case, being aggressive about the purposefulness of my learner's Welsh, including the use of expletives, which placed me firmly in the free-spirited North Wales camp, of which Dewi is the prime mover (and my competition!). Then come back with a romantic, self-deprecating image, identifying myself with the Red Dragon (ddraig goch), the symbol of Wales's indomitable spirit. Next, plagiarize some famous Welsh poetry lines, knowing that will rile many in the audience for sure, and then claim it was my right and duty as an American imperialist poet to do this. Drop in some hip hop (in Welsh, not easy). And finally write "Fy llinell gyntaf o gynghanedd," my first line of cynghanedd, the notoriously complex poetic form of "consonant chime" that only appears in Welsh. Wrap it up with "My big head of dreams"—voila! a STOMP poem! (You'll have to wait till *Language Matters* airs to see how I did—David Grubin insists on drama for the audience!)

Van Gogh's Violin

Ever since Alice Notley assigned our St. Mark's Poetry Project Workshop in 1977 to visit a DeKooning show "and stay there till you write a poem," I've indulged in the light ekphrastic. Being married to Elizabeth Murray sealed the deal. My standard way of working is quick 'n' short in a small notebook, generally one poem per painting, slowly tease the poems out. This has resulted in books: *Beach Simplifies Horizon* (The Grenfell Press, 1998) with black-and-white images by Robert Moskowitz, after Monet's *Bathers,* and *Picasso in Barcelona* (Paper Kite Press, 2011), in the voice of the genius between 14–18, full of talent and testosterone inventing art and sex. Variants include *Cupid's Cashbox* (Jordan Davies, 1988), w/ drawings by Elizabeth Murray, and *A Couple of Ways of Doing Something* (Aperture, 2006), w/ daguerreotypes by Chuck Close. I could barely take my eyes off Van Gogh's paintings to write "Van Gogh's Violin," the way I see him unable to lift his eyes from the celestial to pour on the paint.

Rothkos: Stare at something long enough and it's a poem, and if the form, like Rothko's floating colors, is apparent, I say go for it: Invent Your Own Form. "A poem is a space shot into consciousness," as Bill Knott informed me circa 1672. Late Rothko is trance-inducing, form as tic-tac-toe exercise, brain made of canvas.

How to Write a Rothko:

1. A Rothko (poem) is best written while standing in front of a Rothko (painting).
2. A Rothko is three lines, three words per line.

3. Three of these nine words must be colors, and their position in the poem must be a tic-tac-toe.
4. Like all rules of poetry, break at your own risk.

Urdu Poems: These poems were written for the Poetry Dinners, one of many collaborations between Steve Zeitlin and City Lore and the Bowery Poetry Club/Bowery Arts+Science, where I've been working since 2002— other projects have included the People's Poetry Gathering, the POEMobile, and "Khonsay: A Poem of many Tongues."

"Urdu Poems" were translated originally by Randhir Singh, and I translated them into a more colloquial English with the help of him and the poets. On May 8, 2004, an audience of 100+, most from India and Pakistan, attended a traditional mushaira, a literary gathering where the audience participates by repeating refrains of poems, a pan–South Asian tradition. At this informal mushaira at Shaheen's Sweets restaurant in Jackson Heights, poets sat in a semi-circle on a carpeted stage, with an oil lamp to signal each poet's turn to read. The poets performed original ghazals—lyric, sometimes sung, verses consisting of thematically autonomous couplets unified by rhyme and meter. They read their pieces in Urdu and Punjabi, and both English translations were performed. As is the tradition, the audience chanted "Wa Wa" after lines they enjoyed, and the poets repeated the lines in a call-and-response style—for the English versions as well! Finally, traditional singer Master Niaz, who had also received the poems in advance, sang the lyrics, accompanied by musicians playing tabla drums, harmonium, and the bulbul tarang. The performance was repeated at the People's Poetry Gathering in 2006. I also performed these poems with Lenny Kaye on oud at a Timbila performance at Banjo Jim's.

Immediately Poems (Rilke & Kandinsky): Written while in residence in Munich in 1991. I gave my first reading in New York downstairs at a pizza joint called the Third Phase. Donald Lev hosted; it was 1966.

Jeliya! (or, Griot Poems, As Sung by Alhaji Papa Susso to Bob Holman)
Walter Ong taught me that Orality and Literacy are consciousnesses, not a procession/progression for poetry; Papa Susso taught me that you don't study Orality, you live it. Tom Hale, author of the essential *Griots and Griottes* (Indiana University Press, 1998, 2007) writes: every West African language has a different word for griot, but all of them use *griot*. *Jeli* is the Mandinke word, *jelimussow* if female, and *Jeliya* is the name for the art and practice of the jeli/jelimussow.

My reading lists at the New School and Bard and the Nuyorican were not going over well with the hip hop/spoken word poets. That's when I started trying to read the Hidden Book, as I call it in my introduction to *Aloud: Voices from the Nuyorican Poets Cafe*. It's Hidden because it isn't written down—I'm talking the Oral Tradition. To find it, travel to the place and start asking. Specifically, in 2000, poet/professor/organizer and Eritrean joiner Charles Cantalupo invited me to Against All Odds: African Languages and Literatures into the 21st Century. This extraordinary conference was held in Asmara, Eritrea, where it felt like early Sandanista Nicaragua: a

Poets' Utopia. Among others there: Ngugi wa Thiong'o, Ann Bierstecker, Mblulelo Mzamane, Nawal El Saadawi, Kassahun Checole, Zemhret Yohannes. Eritrea's poet laureate, Reesom Haile; Ararat Iyob; Saba Kidane. That's where I met Papa Susso, and I haven't stopped meeting him since.

I try to keep Papa's spontaneity inside the written. Sometimes I use a single performance as a basis for the whole poem, sometimes I add his comments, and sometimes I work in sections from other voicings of the poem. He wants me to call these works "poems" now. They were "songs" before we met. But listening to Papa—his melodies are speech. His poems talk (and walk). Are these "literal" translations, word-for-word? Unless you write something down you can't memorize it, unless the poet wants you to get it exactly and has you repeat everything over and over, which is the way the Upanishads were handed down, and the Torah, and certain Polynesian poems. Sing this one back to me. Excuse me, Mr. (or Ms.) Homer—could you slow down? I'm scribbling too fast to sing this one back to you . . .

"How Kora Was Born": I'd been listening, i.e., learning from, Papa a couple years. I'd read, reviewed, and taught *Griots and Griottes*. I'd asked Papa to tell me what the songs meant. I asked him if he'd be interested in my actually writing down what he said, working it into a poem, and calling it a poem. Papa didn't think so. Of course, I would read everything back to him to get his approval. No, he still didn't think so, thank you. But he did say it would be fine if he sang and I wrote down what I thought he was saying and then we could perform it together. And that's what we did.

The kora is a twenty-one-stringed harp-lute. It is to Jeliya what the guitar is to rock 'n' roll. The ngoni is a five-stringed Jeliya instrument.

"Jeliya!": Jeliya is the art of the jeli, the life of the jeli. It's like saying "Music(ians)!" After "How Kora Was Born" proved successful in performance,

Papa thought we could try something like a translation, and this was our first. This song calls up all griots, past, present, future. "Jeliya!" was a huge success when we sang it back to his relatives and friends in his hometown village, Sotuma Sere (pop. 1,120).

"Alaleka Jaliyaa Daa!"—Praise God who made Jeliya! These are the languages Papa sings in: Mandinka, Bambara, Fulani, Wolof, Sarahule. He speaks English, French, Spanish, Arabic too.

"Kaira": "Kaira" is performed call-and-response in English, so the audience learns it is the word for "Peace." Papa's "digression" into the story of Kairaba Toure and Teneng Sory Diabate gives the lineage of the poem; it tells the provenance like a "chop" on a Chinese poem/painting.

"Allah L'a Ke": "Allah L'a Ke" is one of the most famous of all Jeliya songs, and the first you learn on the kora. Its tale of fadenya (same-father, different-mother jealousy), is a common theme in jeliya.

"Mandinka in Arabic"—Because the griot languages aren't written, when they are you can use either Arabic or Roman characters.

"Marabout" is a holy person who bridges the Islamic and animist worlds.

"The Loving Father's Song": "jelikuntigi" means "Chief Jeli"

"Manjugalong": Saba Kidane was the hit of the Against All Odds conference (see above). This was the first time she'd ever read publicly, but she took the stage like a pro, "like a rock star," and delivered revolutionary, feminist poetry sans rhetoric but with power and, well, magic. Ngugi and his family formally adopted her. And back in the States, we tried to bring her over for the People's Poetry Gathering. The u.s. consulate said that they would have allowed her to come if she'd been a forty-year-old male with a job and children. Too bad this great poet was twenty-five, female, and a single mother. But the *New York Times* covered the story, and she sent a videotape, so in a way she was present in New York. Manjugalong!

Memory Made Real (or, You Are No Longer Here to Wash Your Hair)
These are personal, family poems, mostly never-before published, about Elizabeth and our children, Dakota, Sophie, Daisy. Elizabeth Murray died in 2007.

"We Met in Managua": Roland Legiardi-Laura wasn't content with his movie on the poetry of the Sandinista revolution (six of the nine members of the ruling council had published books of poetry). So he organized "u.s. Poets Invade Nicaragua!" for the 1988 Dario Festival. Cardenal met us on the tarmac. That was when Pedro Pietri married Diane Burns. Joy Harjo was there, as well as Joe Richey, Kevin Gerien, Zoe Angelsey, Tom Savage, Alurista, Sandy Taylor, Judy Doyle, Jennifer Heath, and Tim Pratt.

"Forget Yesterday": Credit the Beach Boys.

"The Word *Mystery*": *Conversations with Ogotomeli* is by Marcel Griaule OUP, 1975). Nathaniel Mackey's Andamboulou led me to Ogotomeli, who led me to the film I did with the Dogons, centered in Griaule's village, Sangha. "On the Road with Bob Holman, Episode 2," produced by Ram Devineni and Beatriz Seigner-Martin.

"In Passing": About the last thing Elizabeth mentioned seeing were tiny vaporettos in the upper corner of the room. We'd just been to Venice for the Biennale. She noted that Venice was not "wheelchair-friendly."

"To Lisanne": I was writing in the garage in Beverlywood; Lisanne was working on a script in the hall by the washing machine. When I heard her go to Anthony (three months), I wrote the poem. Dakota, my son, was at work. August, Anthony's brother, was observing this quietly—he'd be born the next year. Sonnet.

"In Daisy's Kitchen, Moose Underfoot": Moose is a rescue poodle of the brown variety.

"Day for Sophie and Nick, Epithalamium": Sophia Murray Holman and Nicholas Ellsberg were married at Jan Hashey and Yasuo Minigawa's loft, September 15, 2012. Papa sang at the party, and Vito Ricci and Lys Vachon and I sang this ditty by Holman/Ricci. In Attendance: Daisy Murray Holman, Michael Patrick Walker, and the whole mishpucha.

"Midsummer Kupala": Written for Yara Arts' Ukrainian Midsummer Night Festival. Will be used in *Captain John Smith Goes to Ukraine*, directed by Virlana Tkacz, music by Julian Kytasty.

"Sing This One Back to Me": Performed by Timbila, music by Nora Balaban, guitar solo by Banning Eyre. A fitting conclusion. Pass it on.

COFFEE HOUSE PRESS

Mission

The mission of Coffee House Press is to publish exciting, vital, and enduring authors of our time; to delight and inspire readers; to contribute to the cultural life of our community; and to enrich our literary heritage. By building on the best traditions of publishing and the book arts, we produce books that celebrate imagination, innovation in the craft of writing, and the many authentic voices of the American experience.

Vision

LITERATURE. We will promote literature as a vital art form, helping to redefine its role in contemporary life. We will publish authors whose groundbreaking work helps shape the direction of 21st-century literature. **WRITERS.** We will foster the careers of our writers by making long-term commitments to their work, allowing them to take risks in form and content. **READERS.** Readers of books we publish will experience new perspectives and an expanding intellectual landscape. **PUBLISHING.** We will be leaders in developing a sustainable 21st-century model of independent literary publishing, pushing the boundaries of content, form, editing, audience development, and book technologies.

Values

Innovation and excellence in all activities
Diversity of people, ideas, and products
Advancing literary knowledge
Community through embracing many cultures
Ethical and highly professional management and governance practices

Good books are brewing at coffeehousepress.org

Funder acknowledgment

Coffee House Press is an independent, nonprofit literary publisher. Our books are made possible through the generous support of grants and gifts from many foundations, corporate giving programs, state and federal support, and through donations from individuals who believe in the transformational power of literature. Coffee House Press receives major operating support from Amazon, the Bush Foundation, the Jerome Foundation, the McKnight Foundation, from Target, and in part from a grant provided by the Minnesota State Arts Board through an appropriation by the Minnesota State Legislature from the State's general fund and its arts and cultural heritage fund with money from the vote of the people of Minnesota on November 4, 2008, and a grant from the Wells Fargo Foundation of Minnesota. Support for this title was received from the National Endowment for the Arts, a federal agency. Coffee House also receives support from: several anonymous donors; Suzanne Allen; Elmer L. and Eleanor J. Andersen Foundation; Around Town Agency; Patricia Beithon; Bill Berkson; the E. Thomas Binger and Rebecca Rand Fund of the Minneapolis Foundation; the Patrick and Aimee Butler Family Foundation; Ruth Dayton; Dorsey & Whitney, LLP; Mary Ebert and Paul Stembler; Chris Fischbach and Katie Dublinski; Fredrikson & Byron, P.A.; Sally French; Anselm Hollo and Jane Dalrymple-Hollo; Jeffrey Hom; Carl and Heidi Horsch; Alex and Ada Katz; Stephen and Isabel Keating; Kenneth Kahn; the Kenneth Koch Literary Estate; Kathy and Dean Koutsky; the Lenfestey Family Foundation; Carol and Aaron Mack; Mary McDermid; Sjur Midness and Briar Andresen; the Nash Foundation; the Rehael Fund of the Minneapolis Foundation; Schwegman, Lundberg & Woessner, P.A.; Kiki Smith; Jeffrey Sugerman and Sarah Schultz; Patricia Tilton; the Archie D. & Bertha H. Walker Foundation; Stu Wilson and Mel Barker; the Woessner Freeman Family Foundation; Margaret and Angus Wurtele; and many other generous individual donors.

ART WORKS.
arts.gov

MINNESOTA
STATE ARTS BOARD

TARGET.

amazon.com

To you and our many readers across the country,
we send our thanks for your continuing support.

Colophon

Sing This One Back to Me was designed at Coffee House Press,
in the historic Grain Belt Brewery's Bottling House
near downtown Minneapolis.
Fonts include Garamond and Futura.